CELLO FOR KIDS

CELLO FOR KIDS

Christmas Carols, Classical Music, Nursery Rhymes, Traditional & Folk Songs!

CELLO FOR KIDS:

Christmas Carols, Classical Music, Nursery Rhymes, Traditional & Folk Songs!

ISBN-13:978-1499243420
ISBN-10:1499243421

Contents

Playing guide

Standard notation

Notes are written on a Staff.

Staff

The staff consists of five lines and four spaces, on which notes symbols are placed.

Clef

A clef assigns an individual note to a certain line. The **Bass Clef** or **F Clef** is used for the cello.

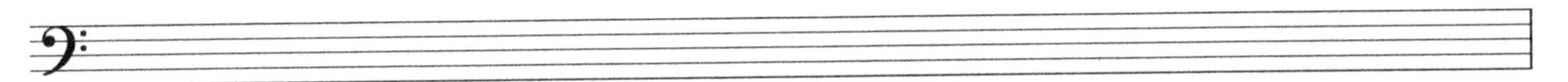

This clef indicates the position of the note F which is on the line between the two dots.

Note

A note is a sign used to represent the relative pitch of a sound. There are seven notes: A, B, C, D, E, F and G.

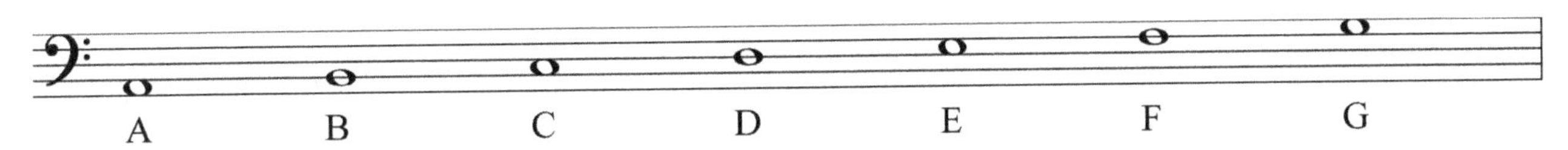

Ledger lines

The ledger lines are used to inscribe notes outside the lines and spaces of the staff.

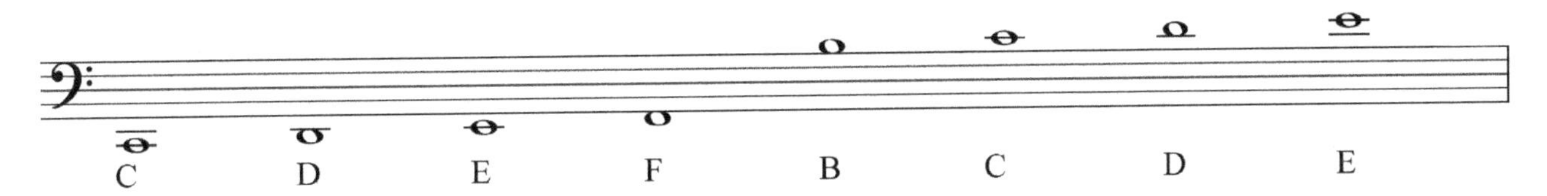

Accidentals

An accidental is a symbol to raise or lower the pitch of a note.

♯ sharp	Next note up half step.
♭ flat	Next note down half step.
♮ natural	Cancels a flat or a sharp.

Note values

A **note value** is used to indicate the duration of a note. A **rest** is an interval of silence, marked by a sign indicating the length of the pause. Each rest corresponds to a particular note value.

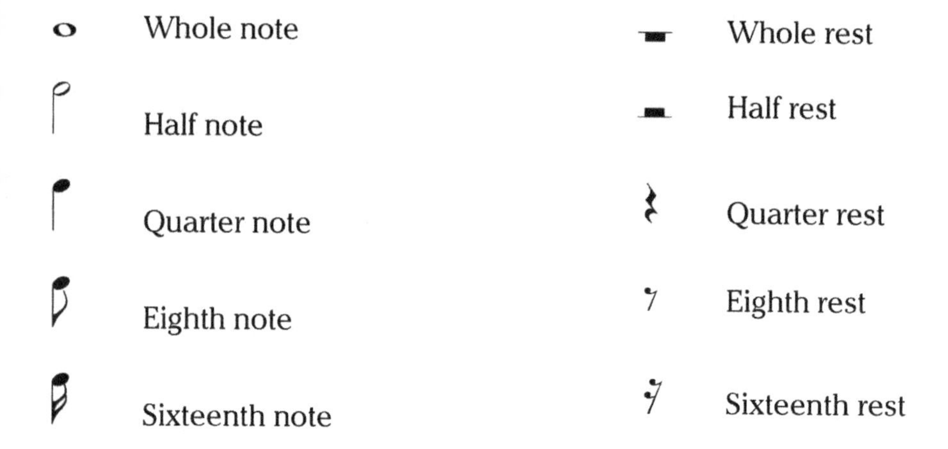

Dotted note

A dotted note is a note with a small dot written after it. The dot adds half as much again to the basic note's duration.

Tie

A tie is a curved line connecting the heads of two notes of the same pitch, indicating that they are to be played as a single note with a duration equal to the sum of the individual notes' note values.

Bars or Measures

The staff is divided into equal segments of time consisting of the same number of beats, called bar or measures.

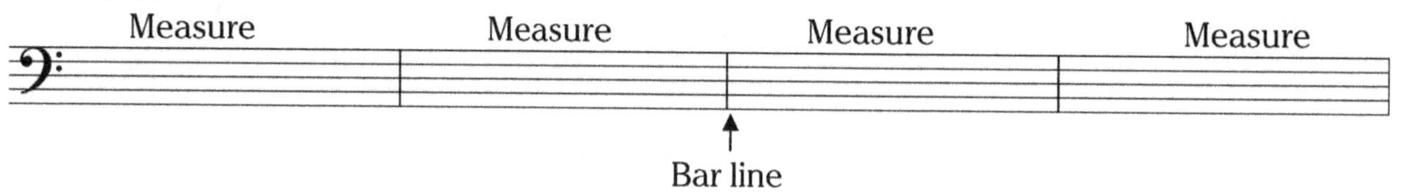

Time signature

Time signature consists of two numbers, the upper number specifies how many beats (or counts) are in each measure, and the lower number tells us the note value which represents one beat.

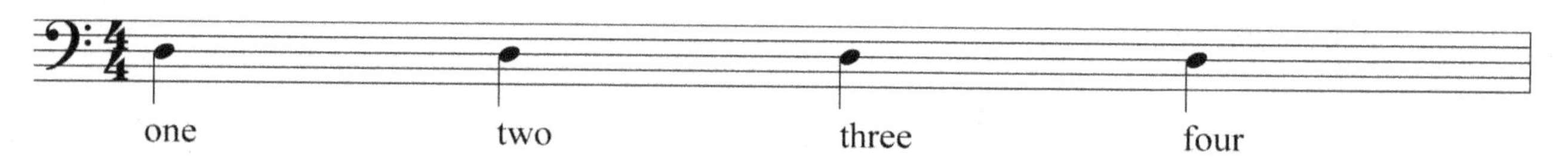

Example: 4/4 means four quarters, or four beats per measure with a quarter note receiving one beat or count.

Key signature

A Key signature is a group of accidentals, generally written at the beginning of a score immediately after the clef, and shows which notes always get sharps or flats. Accidentals on the lines and spaces in the key signature affect those notes throughout the piece unless there is a natural sign.

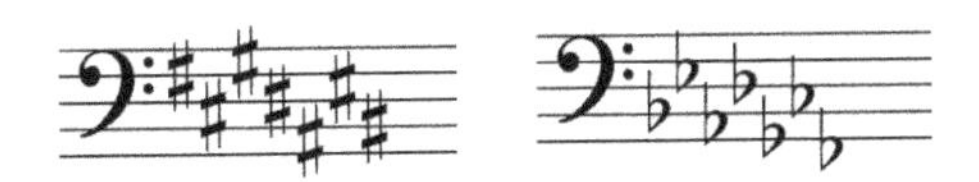

Repeat sign

The repeat sign indicates a section should be repeated from the beginning, and then continue on. A corresponding sign facing the other way indicates where the repeat is to begin.

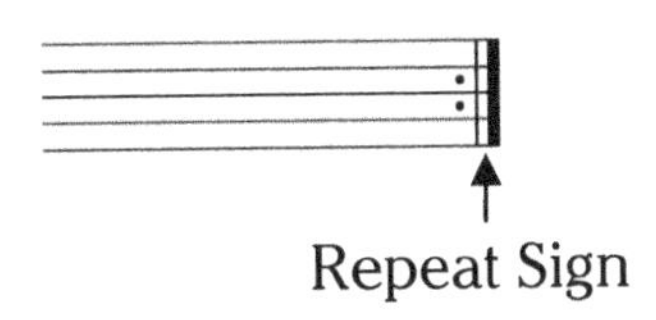

First and second endings

The section should be repeated from the beginning, and number brackets above the bars indicate which to played the first time (1), which to play the second time (2).

Dynamics

Dynamics refers to the volume of the notes.

p (piano), meaning soft.
mp (mezzo-piano), meaning "moderately soft".
mf (mezzo-forte), meaning "moderately loud".
f (forte), meaning loud.

Crescendo. A gradual increase in volume.
Decrescendo. A gradual decrease in volume.

Tempo Markings

Tempo is written at the beginning of a piece of music and indicates how slow or fast this piece should be played.

Adagio — slow and stately (66–76 bpm)
Andate — at a walking pace (76–108 bpm)
Moderato — moderately (101-110 bpm)
Allegro — fast, quickly and bright (120–139 bpm)
Allegretto — moderately fast (but less so than allegro)
Presto — extremely fast (180–200 bpm)

Articulation

Legato. Notes are played smoothly and connected.

Stacatto. Notes are played separated or detached from its neighbours by a silence.

Fermata (pause)
The note is to be prolonged at the pleasure of the performer.

Fingering

In this book left hand fingering is indicated using numbers above the staff.
0= open
1= index
2= middle
3= ring
4= little finger

Bowings

Down-bow

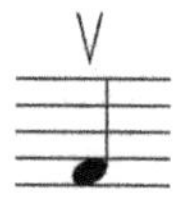

Up-bow

Slur

Indicates that two or more notes are to be played in one bow.

Aloutte

Traditionnel

Amazing Grace

Traditional

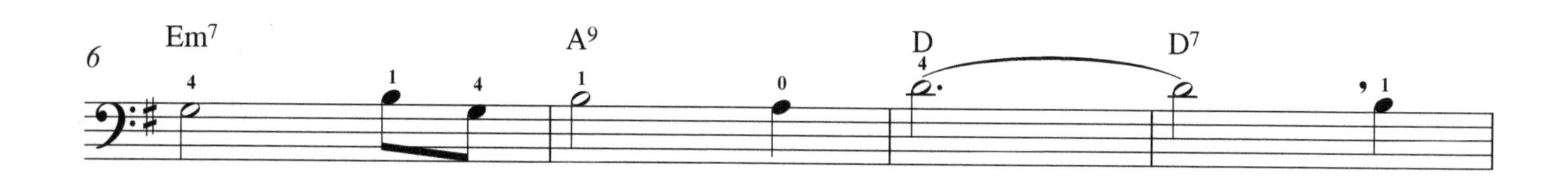

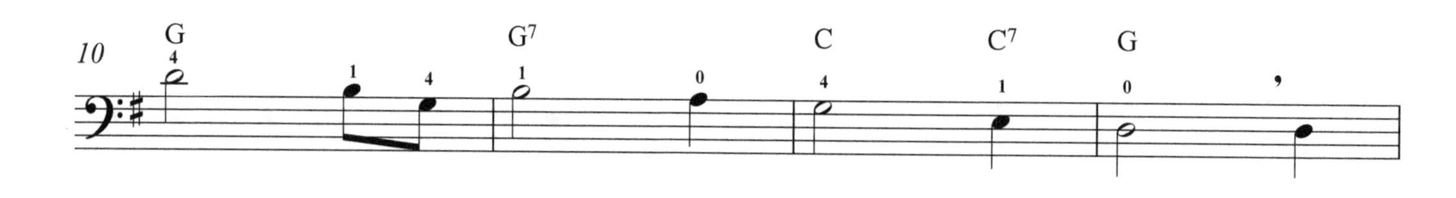

America The Beautiful

Music by Samuel A. Ward

Moderato

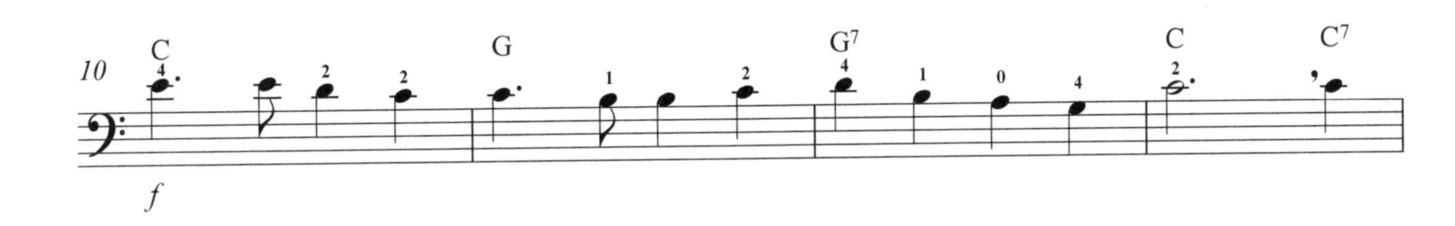

Arroz Con Leche

Tradicional

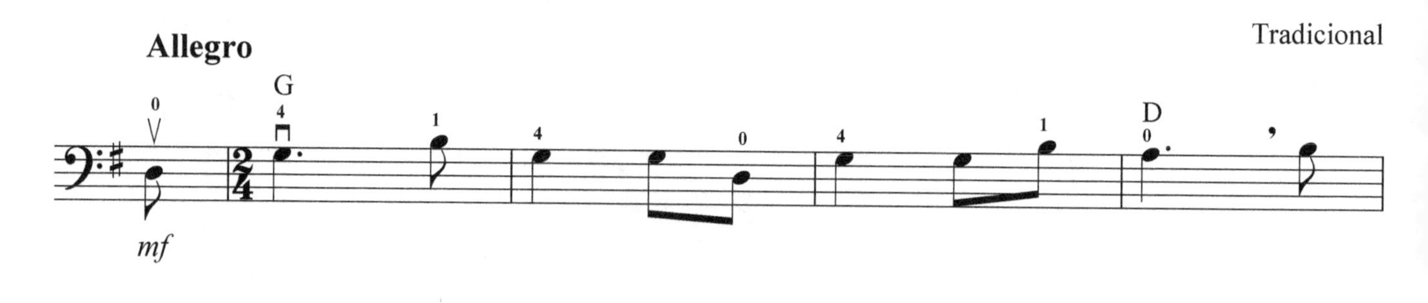

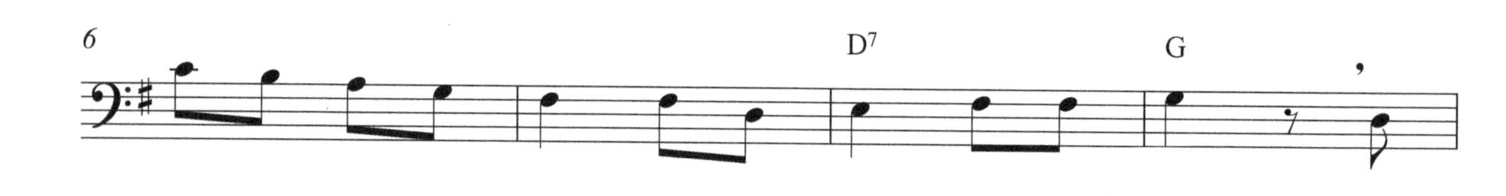

Aserrín, Aserrán

Tradicional

Aura Lee

George R. Poulton

Allegro

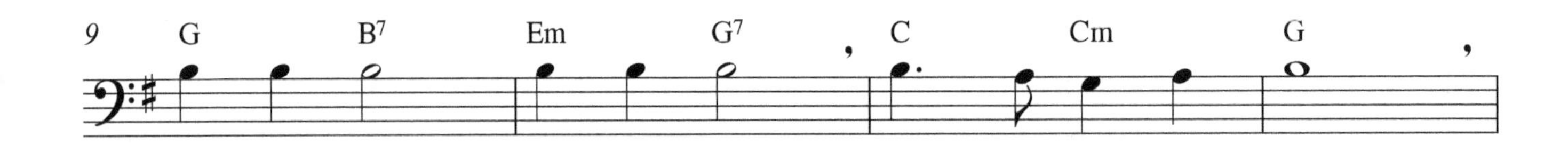

Cielito Lindo

Quirino Mendoza y Cortés

For He's a Jolly Good Fellow

Frere Jacques

Traditionnel

Go Tell Aunt Rhody

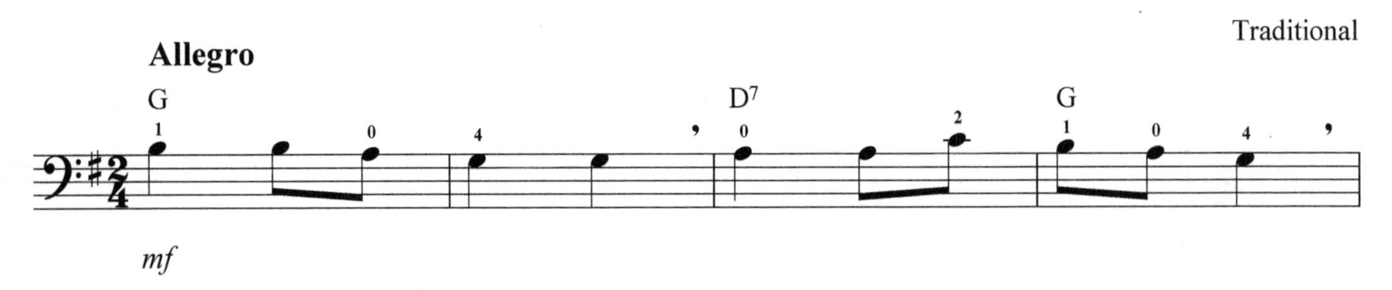

Good Morning To All

Patty & Mildred J. Hill

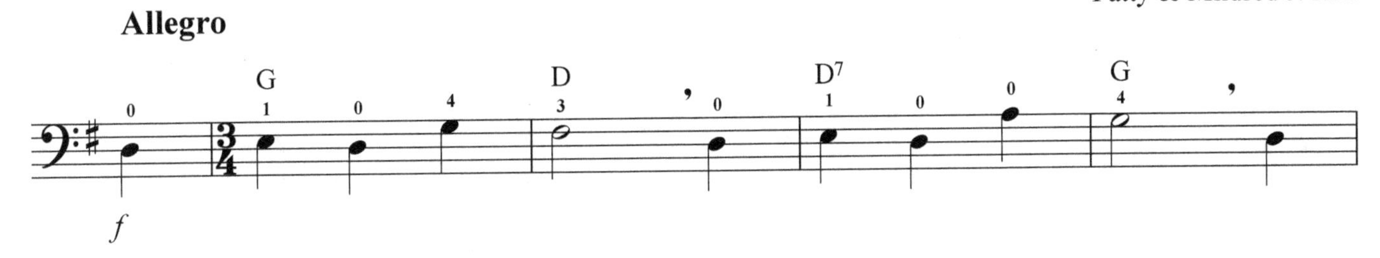

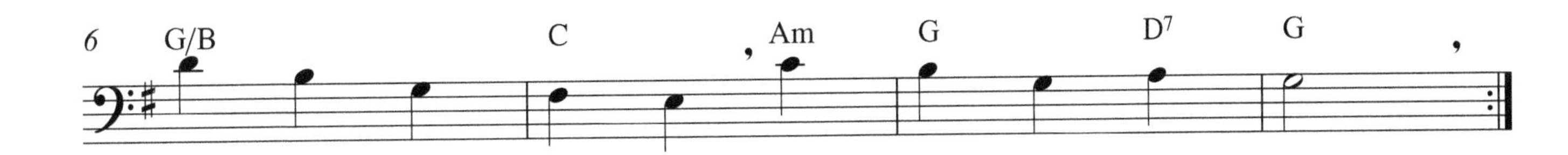

Greensleeves

Jingle Bells

James Lord Pierpont

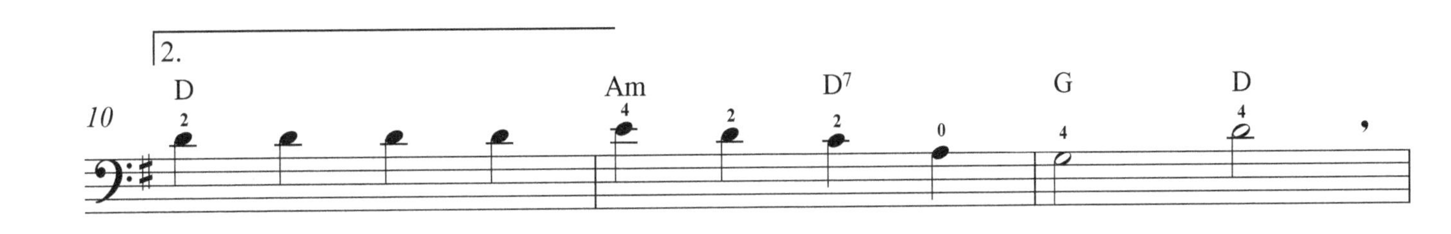

La Cucaracha

Allegro

Tradicional

La Donna è Mobile

Giuseppe Verdi

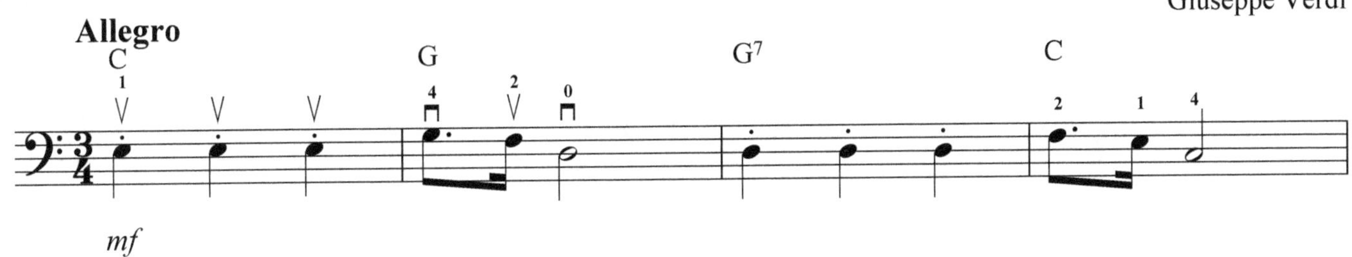

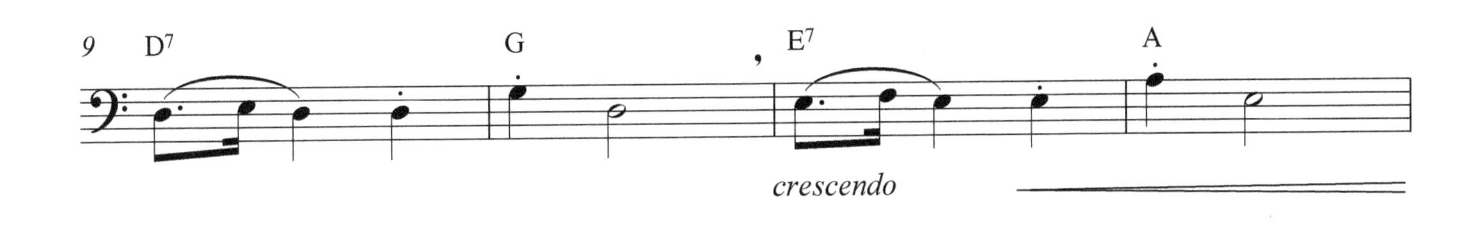

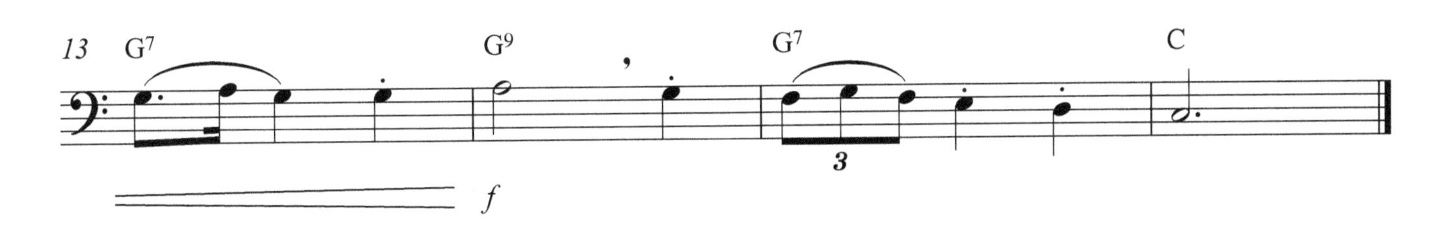

Las Mañanitas

Tradicional

London Bridge Is Falling Down

Traditional

Allegro

D A D

0 1 0 4 3 4 0 1 3 4 1 4 0

mf

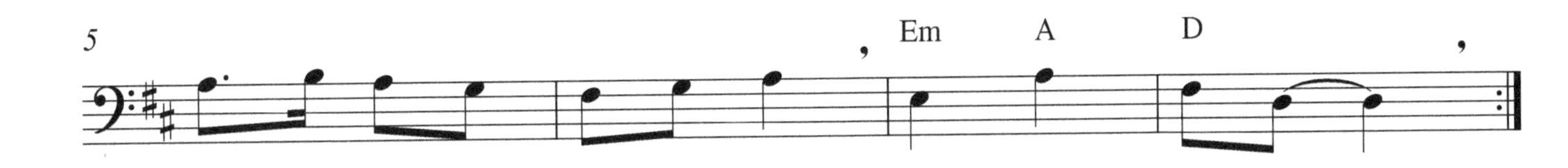

Mary Had A Little Lamb

Menuett

Johann Sebastian Bach

Allegretto

My Bonnie Lies Over The Ocean

Ode an die Freude

Ludwig Van Beethoven

Moderato

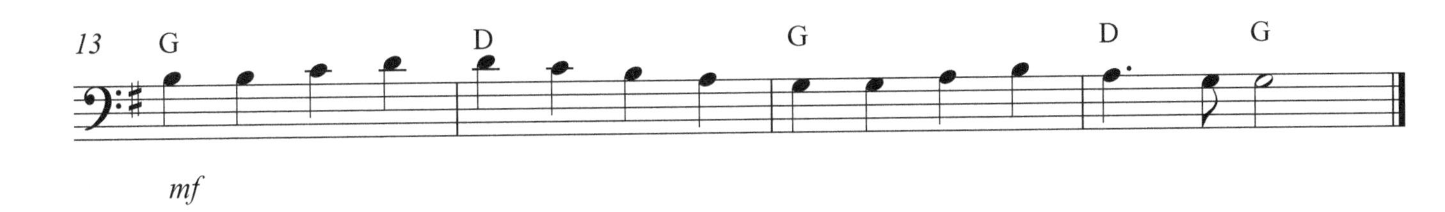

Oh! Susanna

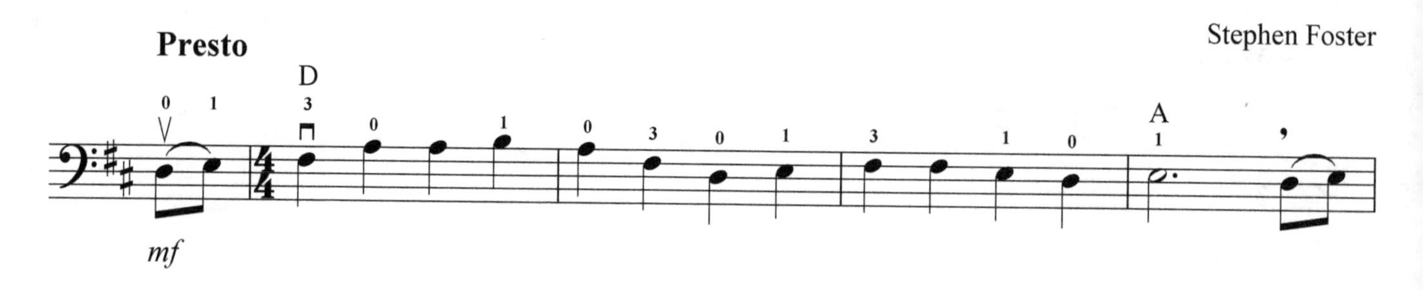

Old MacDonald Had A Farm

Traditional

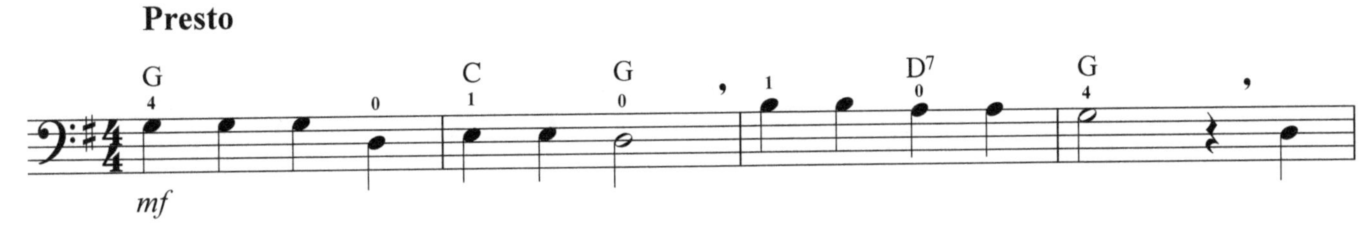

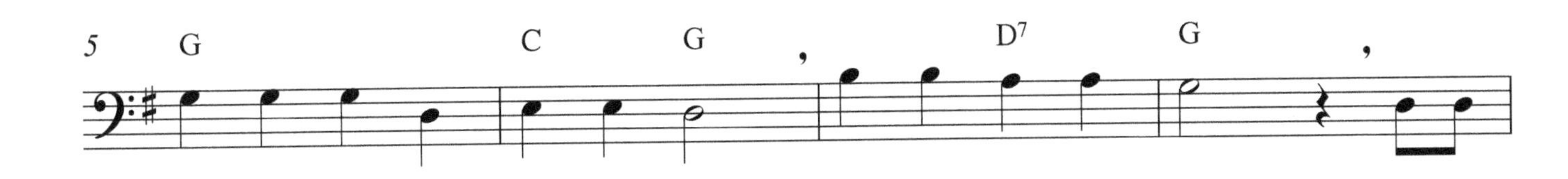

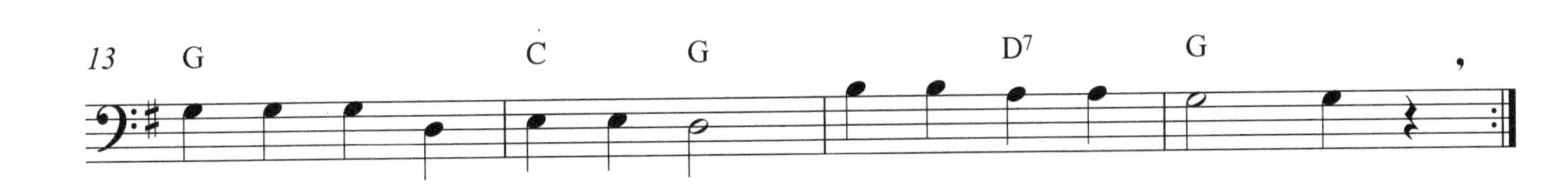

Row Row Row Your Boat

Scarborough Fair

Traditional

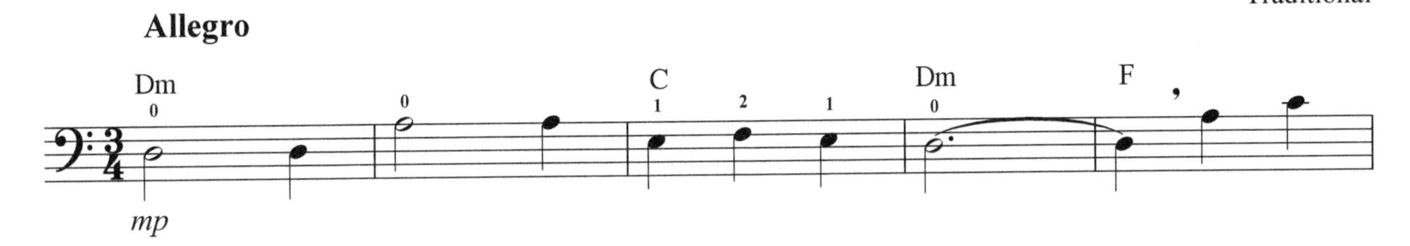

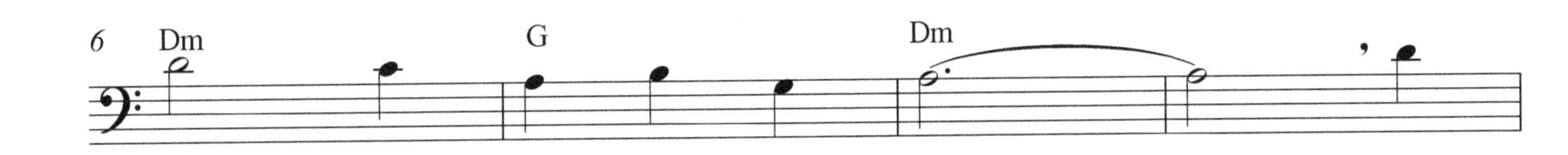

Stille Nacht, heilige Nacht

Franz Xaver Gruber

Sur le Pont d'Avignon

Traditionnel

Allegro

G D G D

4 0 1 2 4 4 3 4 0 0

mf

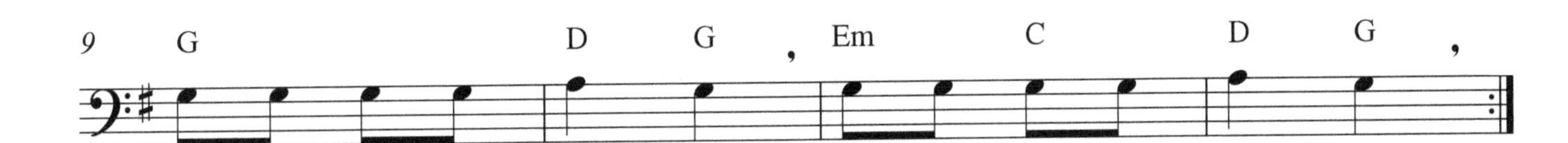

The House Of The Rising Sun

Traditional

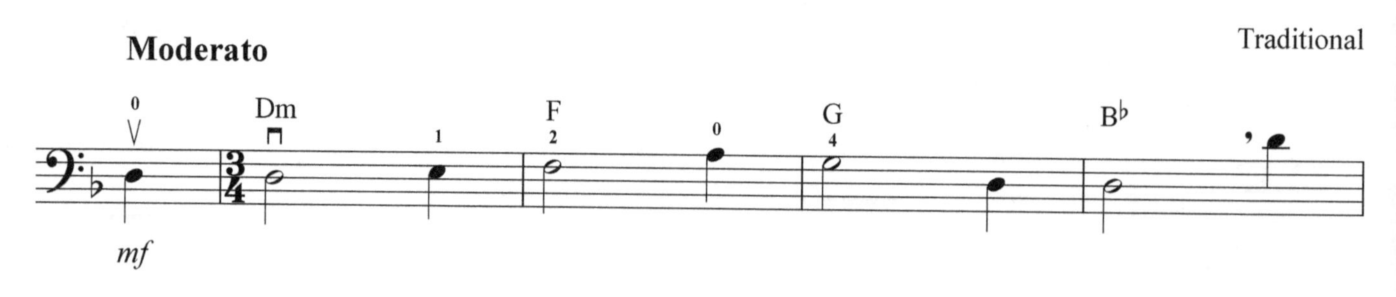

The Star-Spangled Banner

Music by John Stafford Smith

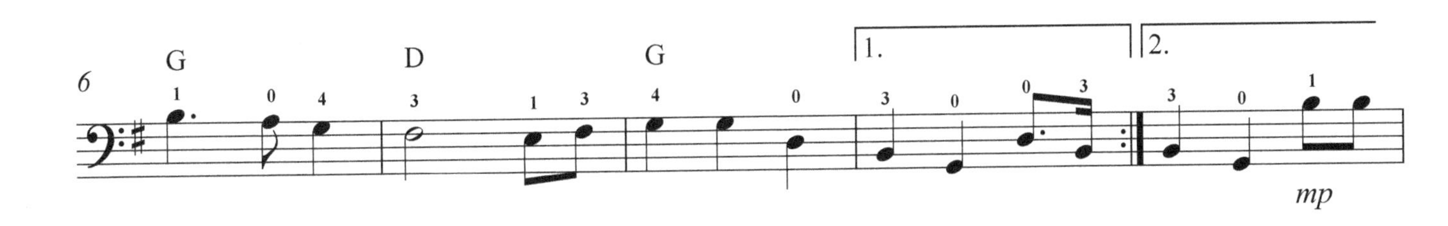

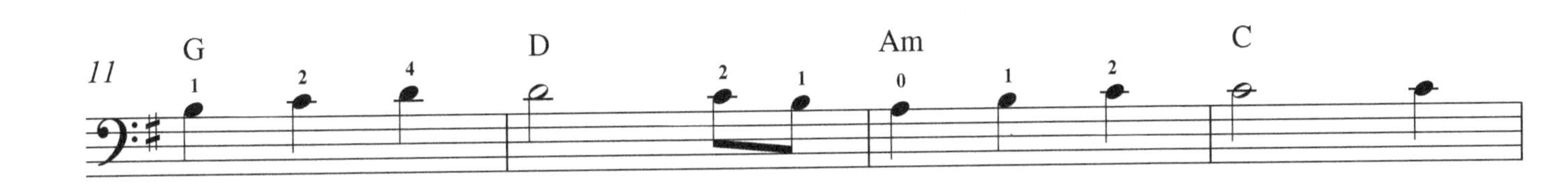

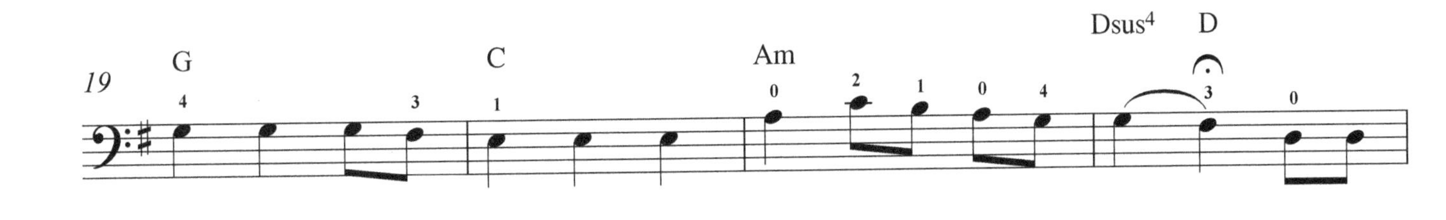

Twinkle Twinkle Little Star

W. A. Mozart

Moderato

D Bm Bm7 G D A D

0 0 1 0 4 3 1 0

mf

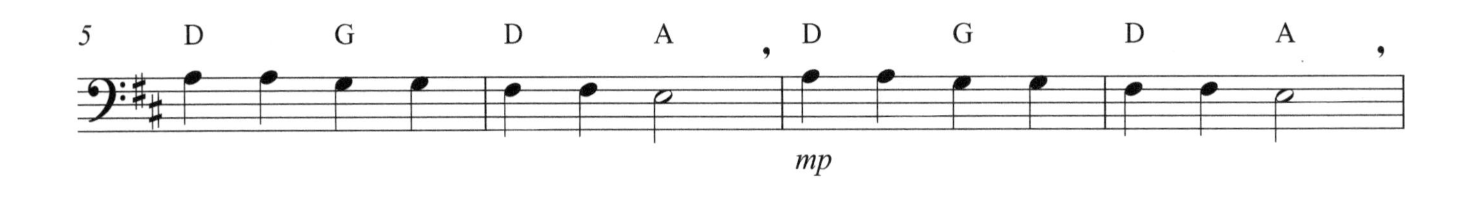

Un Elefante Se Balanceaba

Tradicional

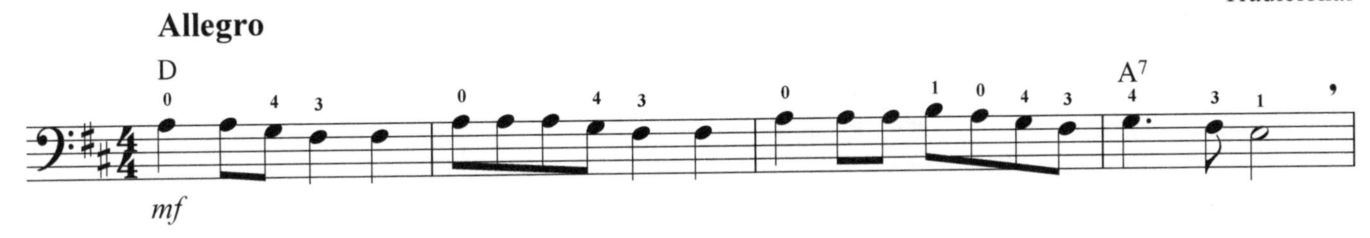

We Wish You A Merry Christmas

Presto

Traditional

When Johnny Comes Marching Home

Traditional

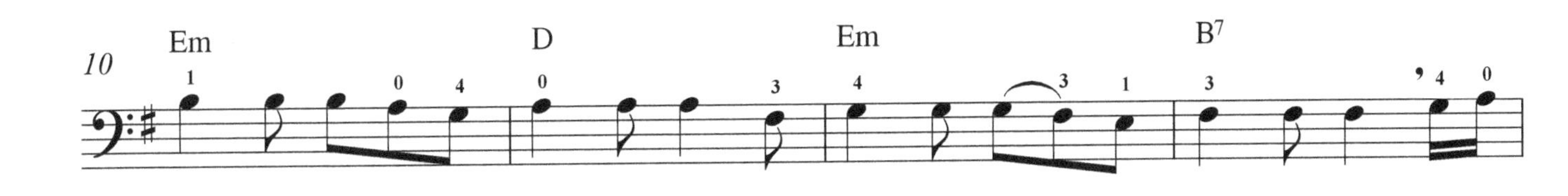

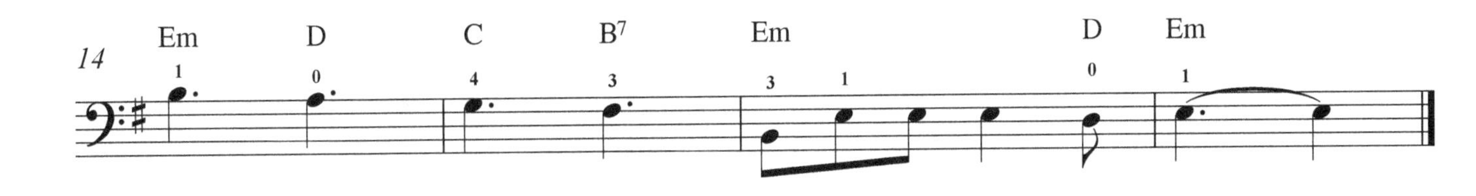

When The Saints Go Marching In

Presto

Traditional

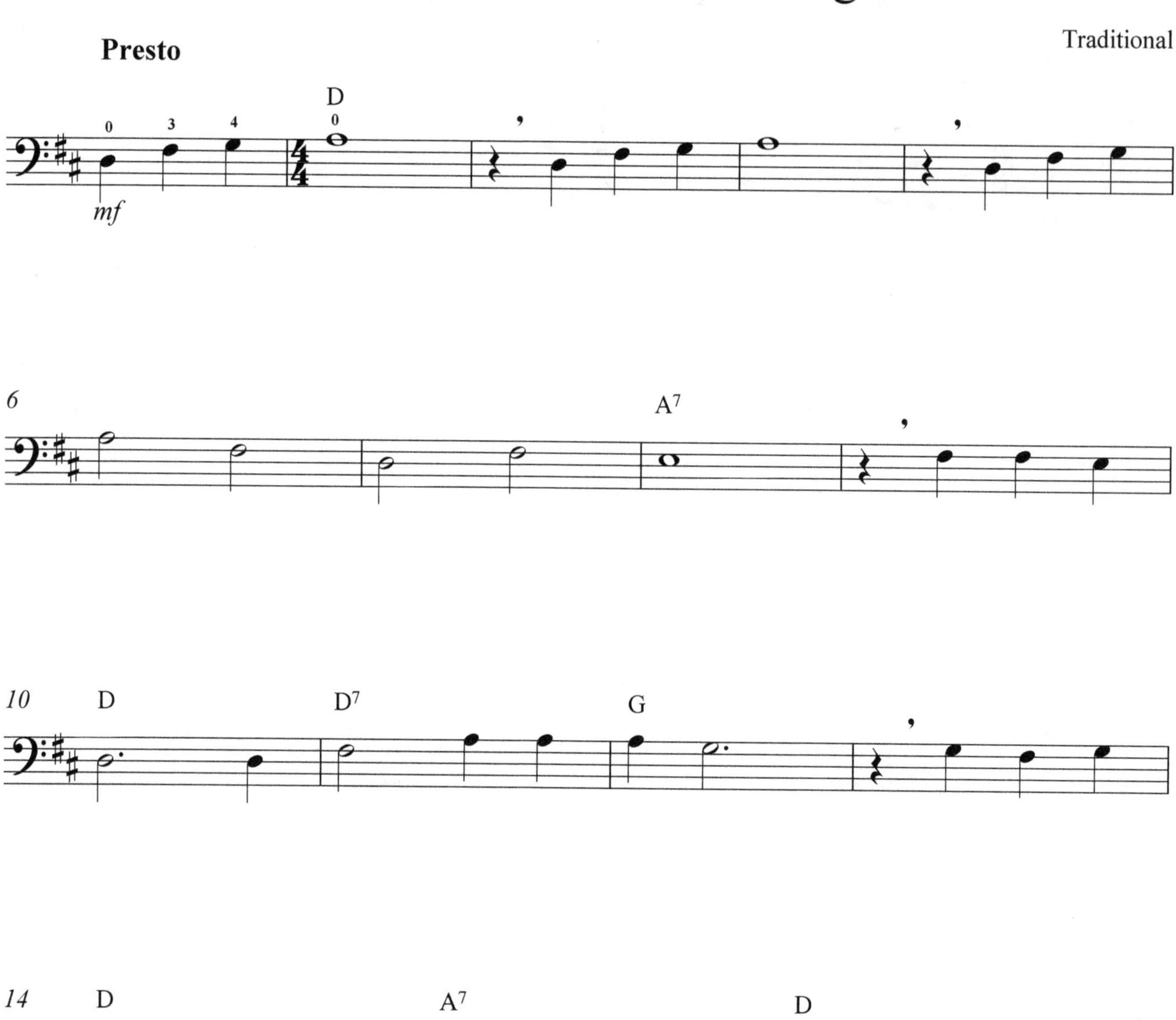

Wiegenlied

Johannes Brahms

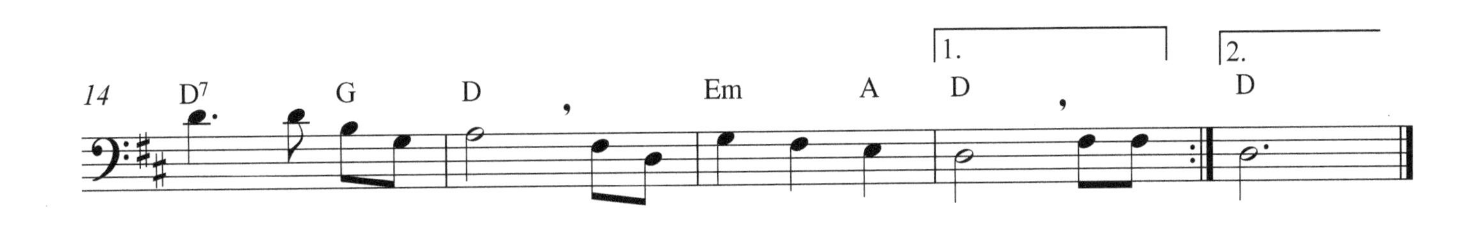

Yankee Doodle

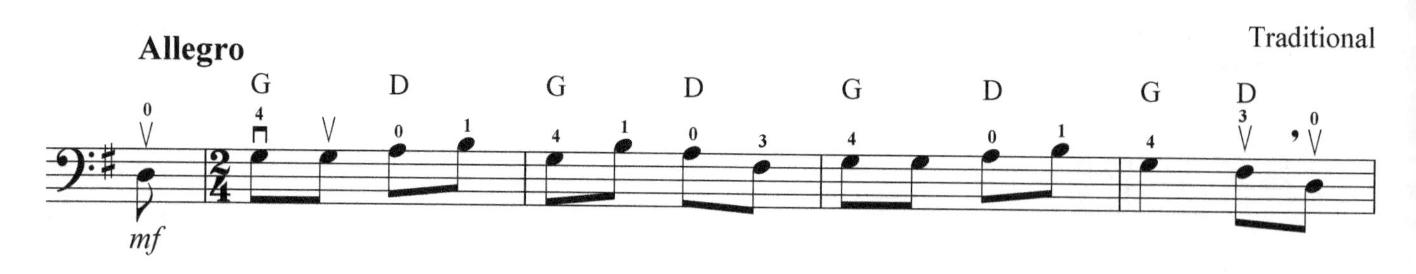

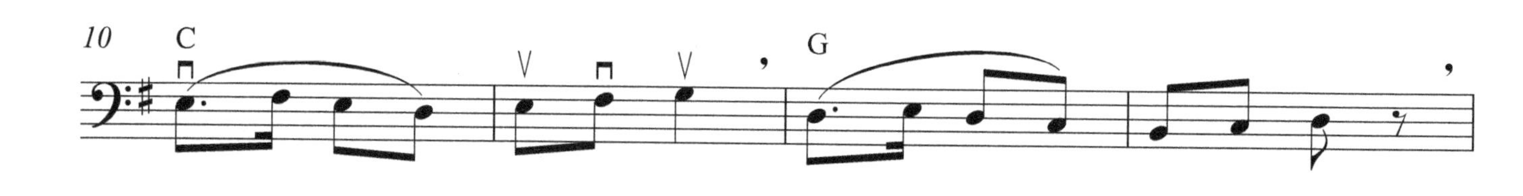

info@marcomusica.com

CPSIA information can be obtained
at www.ICGtesting.com
Printed in the USA
LVHW062218181118
597597LV00018B/452/P